Sŵn y Morloi

Hannah Stone

Maytree Press 2019

Published 2019 by Maytree Press

www.maytreepress.org

Copyright © Hannah Stone 2019

ISBN: 978-1-9160381-0-3

A CIP catalogue record of this book is available from the British Library.

Cover image: The Sound of Seals © David Coldwell

Printed in the UK by PiggyPrint

Maytree 001

Contents

Abergwaun I. Soldiers, 1797

What seas, what shores, what excitement
in the Royal Oak, when the surrender
is signed by the last invaders,

bedraggled in breeches and tricorns,
dragging their hangovers; faces red
as the petticoats swirled

by goodwife Jemima
and sturdy sisters –
no menfolk about

to fight the Frenchies
that swarmed like the rats
off their ships, scrambling up

from Carragwastad,
leaving their frigate undefended,
waves lapping its empty bulwarks.

Abergwaun II. Another Invasion

What seas, what shores, what streams
of loud people visiting,
with film scripts, dimming the mist

with hot white lights,
tempers flaring in the bar,
catching now fish, now fame,

fake whales, false hopes,
gone in a flash when the crew packs up
leaving the locals to quiet pints,

and contemplation of the dark track
from station to ferry terminal,
two trains a day, change at Carmarthen.

Abergwaun III. Memories

Raymond Lewis (1915-2009): Happy memories as I go thither, my final way, the way to the sea.
Molly Lewis (1924-2012): Who can fear the God who made the rose?

They marked the place with memories
which warm the bench you sit on
to catch your breath
(it is a sharp climb from the Lower Town).
The roses are not yet in bud,
but primroses hold up golden hearts
above soft blades of grass,
and a song bird strings its notes
like pearls on a wisp of mist.
Where people have left love,
there is more than sea air to inhale.

Nanhyfer – a digression via St Non's

The cuckoo is a cheat,
the priest a gull who believes
she will return next spring in time for Mass.
But wait he did, and that April day
two deaths he marked,
his Lord who rose again,
the bird whose flight fluttered
its last on the altar.

'See,' she said,
'your blooded man hung on the tree
is also a cuckoo; squatting
in settlements built by the first
to place these stones as homes for faith.
Now, ivy ribbons their temples,
and my end is near.'

Brynach's legend glows
through coloured windows
in the chapel of St Non.
The cuckoo's days are numbered,
the old chapel in pieces,
but the new altar holds together
the Petrine commission:

Strumble Head is my rock,
and on this rock will I worship the wind,
and give thanks for the waves.

Pant y Dŵr

Chthonic eyes see slugs on gravel.
Sea senses read seals on shingle,
watch the up-rearing heads
and tail-end of vanishing tricks.
It takes the best part of a week
to learn the guile of buoys bobbing in bays,
anchoring attention to their masquerade.
It is the best part of the week
when black blobs fail to fool you,
and, looking with sharpened sight,
you glimpse whiskers above waves,
the shoreward gaze of round eyes
inviting a second glance.

Aber Felin I. Llanwnda

The air thrums with legends.
Bells commemorating drowned sailors
ring in the flock of St. Gwyndaf,
urge folk to pass the antics of ewes and their young,
button up their tweed jackets,
and come and celebrate the risen Lamb.

Clouds dance with the sun.

Midweek, a funereal toll snags mist
round the dolmen,
and you could believe the story
about the white dog that appears
beside the rocky tomb,
unseen by the millennial collie.

Ivy veins the tilted roof-space.

Its roots reach for ley lines, tugging at rituals
we can only guess at.
In the graveyard below,
Easter's coloured threads are shunned.
Decent black coats post
a row of crows beside the hearse.

Aber Felin II. Easter on the Edge

The festival bells peel inland.
Beside the church, car doors slam,
greetings cheer the chilly air,
while on the headland
wind winnows the bay.
Yellow archangel announces
imminent rebirth, and,
in the hedgerow,
a lattice of small thorns
swell in bud.
Each flower will offer
one white petal
for every one of His wounds.

Penrhyn

"Two star cottage. No electricity precludes higher grade."

The cottage makes its own acoustics.
Cast-iron stove throws off clicks;
its charge of logs pop and whine.
Soft breaths whisper up the funnel of oil lamps;
matches scratch and flare as they catch
the wick of candles placed beside the open book,
where, biscuit in hand, the boy devours pictures
from *Collins' Guide to Birds*. Mouths 'Chough'
as he spider-writes a date and grid ref.
Chews the syllables of its other-tongued name –
'Brân Goesgoch.'
His sister's eyes are red-riding-hood-wide
as she recites all she has learned about sea otters.
At night, the wind rocks their duvet nests in the crog loft,
murmurs tomorrow's secrets into the shells of their ears.

Porthsychan

wind is pinned briefly,
reclaimed as seals giving voice,
sounding from the bay

not dogs nor children
yapping, crying, calling out,
but beached seals barking

Carreg Onnen

You can practice mindfulness on an upright chair
and a troop of unwelcome mounts
canter through the stable door:
Broodmare takes the lead,
followed by Mona, while Hope lags in the rear.
You're instructed to observe
the rise and fall of your abdomen.
Feel the steel embrace of ribs round each breath.

Bit, bridle, martingale.

Or try it here, where the wind rides out.
Balance on the headland,
and sync heartbeat to lighthouse.
Flash, wait. Flash, wait, wait.
Flash.
Count the wild ponies crunching gorse.
Follow the sway of their manes with quiet eyes,
self-soothe by listing the colours you see;

Brindle, chestnut, palomino.

Pwll Deri I. Framed

Seabirds calling for the wind,
black cows mud-mired in ruddy fields,
the cycle of the lighthouse beam,
a promise of seals on stony shores –

here are the corner pieces
for the jigsaw of Swn y Morloi cottage.

Each evening, over the dinner table,
a different picture framed
in a deep cut window – a sunset glazed,
or mist, eluding capture by lens and brush.

Pwll Deri II. Gwestai

The hill above my rented home
is just called 'big' on the map,
and, cheek by jowl, in gothic script,
an enigmatic 'fort' is marked.

Seagulls are king of this castle,
a comfortless bastion unroofed by clouds,
a perch for Allied troops watching for the Bosch;
welcome windbreak for walkers.

Below me, smoke rises from the chimney
of Sŵn y Morloi cottage –
the stove is temperamental,
but the farm cats welcoming,

and Ginger himself waits on the doorstep
to invite me to take the best seat in the house;
it's time to sip a glass of wine,
and watch the sun quench itself in the Irish Sea.

Aber Bach hosts a holiday

Tidal as a planet with too many moons,
the coast pulls groups for their annual break.

Lovers, parents tired by the new baby,
three-generational clusters, outdoor lads.

They're drawn to the shingle, where the millrace hastens
to release its bubbles into the brine.

The evening licks last light along the horizon.
Sleeked by immersion, two heads bob on the waves,

one human, one canine, both vocal
as they spill limbs onto the beach.

Feet, webbed in swim socks, and paws
pattern the smooth face of the sand.

At night the cottages bloat with noise;
electronics are charged, and glasses recharged.

Salt water drips from neoprene skins
sagging on rope lines by the cars.

The tide comes in, stacks the shale slope,
tidies the fringe of weeds. Swallows

gristly webs of fishing net,
spits up twine-tangles, tin cans.

The wind makes mouth music with the day's debris.

Melin Tregwynt – a spin-off

At the loom, a woman loads the warp onto the creel,
hopes to finish threading in by tea-time.
The stream has flooded the ford;
children shriek, and shove each other
across the narrow bridge.
Pester power just about queues in the cafe.
A rainbow of spools feeds the eye;
folded bales of finished fabric
call out to the wallet; it seems strange
to see these hedgerow colours under cover.

Evening falls after a sunless day,
layering greys like doublecloth.
Walking back from Aber Bach, I stop to help a ewe.
She has woven her fleece into the hedge,
a strand of barbed wire winds tightly.
Though I try to play God, untangling
her greasy coat from its grip,
with each move she locks herself
faster in the hedge, Isaac's ransom
to her fretful lamb who calls through the mist.

Aber Mawr

Arnold heard the 'grating roar'
of pebbles clawing at the beach.
My ship of faith sailed long ago,
and on the shingle shore I listen
to stirred stones whispering to the waves
which seek to make them sand.

'Rather than burden your craft with doctrine,
use jetsam and flotsam
to piece together a raft light enough
to cling to the meniscus between hope and doubt.
Waste nothing. Use this soft-edged slab of glass,
that stem of seaweed,
even the crumpled crisp packet and solitary sock.
Do not ask for a compass.'

Beacon – a diversion

Boots know the route home;
they are stoical about roads that climb
from the coast path, steering you
along the upward curves
which hone your hamstrings.

It's dusk, but there are prompts. Lamps
shine from cottage windows; headlights
duck and dive along the lanes
where Amazon and Asda routes
have swallowed up the ley lines.

A short diversion down a track
leads to this disc suspended
in the darkening sky, where
pilots navigate by signs
pedestrians cannot grasp.

Its cone of confusion
pinpoints locations for airmen,
a vortex of jumbled signals
which map the skies
for those in the know.

Leaving the beacon behind,
you're nearly back now,
feet tingling at the prospect
of dry socks; will one match
catch the kindling today?

You think of those for whom
the radar broadcasts nothing.
Absence gnaws at morsels of hope
still clutched. Arms lifted *orans*
transmit only grief to deaf deities.

Ty-Croes – an interlude

This morning, take a rain check.
The window's streaked with rivulets;
coffee aroma rises from a mug. A snail
works its way to the top of the pane.

It labours, this mollusc;
muscles clench, feelers flicker in and out
as it ascends. Its shell is fine as Chippendale.
By the coaster on the window sill,
the relics of a small death.

Overnight, a moth folded its damask wings
into a downy scrap of tapestry;
it rises and falls in the draught.

Abercastle

Was it mid-day when you landed?
Burly men gripped your aching limbs
as you splashed into the shallows,
and there was bunting, and cheering,
and your hand was pumped
by every man-jack of the crowd.
There was a brass-band playing
'Land of our Fathers', and gnats' piss beer
in pewter tankards, served from a barrel
brought down from the Trefin hotel,
with a buxom girl twisting the brass tap
in red, raw fingers, and dogs barking,
and snot-snouted lads shoving each other:
'take a message to the telegraph office, mister?
The pony and trap's waiting.'

Or was it dawn, with no reception
but retired Ableseaman Billy Pritchard?
He was watching the tide fill up the harbour,
tamping down his first pipe of the day,
and shifting his peg-leg off the bench.
He raised his tweed cap to you, and asked:
'Is it good crabs, where you come from, then?'
And all you wanted was to be still,
to no longer feel the deck ducking and diving,
to hear the waves slapping the shingle,
to see something that wasn't sea-blue
or mist-grey or cloud-white –
that burst of gorse on the cliff,
the flags of ragged robin fluttering in the hedge,
even the yellow spirals of a landsnail's shell.

Careg Sampson

Surely something is trapped here,
where tractors hem the selvage
of grass round the burial chamber.

Slabbed roof and uprights are freighted with purpose,
the whole site jealous of the liberties taken
by breezes blowing inshore between the stones.

It seems impertinent
to look through the gap
for a sea view to wrap this sight in,

as if admiring the sun's dalliance
with clouds might cause amnesia
about the lives buried here,

beneath rock, beneath sod, earthed
in rites old and lost as their bones,
hidden in antique fonts on the map.

Pwll Ofla

Here is a circle of stone stubs in a meadow,
staking the headland between gull's cliff-top screaming,
and the buzz of strimmers neatening field into lawn.

If they were mushrooms, you'd call them a fairy ring.

Too small to steer sailors, they chart other journeys
(the sturdy-booted hiker, striding up from the village,
rests a hand on one, as if it were a trig point),

or they tell stories of smaller people,
with naked feet, who levered them upright
under stars whose light only now makes its way to earth.

Abereiddi

'In the interest of Health and Safety, no changing of wetsuits in these toilets'

Gracious harbour,
sharing your azure depths
with limpets in wetsuits,
arthritic Labradors
doing doggy paddle,
sunblocked toddlers
first-footing the shallows.

Insatiate sea,
you only took
what was yours
after we had ripped the slate
from your cliffs,
and pierced the sides
with tramlines.

Sensible National Park,
requesting we place
our devices *just here*
and email the photos
to help them record
how the coastline
is changing.

Harbour cottages,
who will now
shake sand in your corners,
steam up the windows
with homecoming brews,
open the door
to the keening of gulls?

Whitesands

In the time it takes for the espresso machine
to fuss froth onto a cappuccino, it's been and gone.

Clouds storm over Garn Llydi,
burst on the beach bouncing raindrops big as pebbles.

Then sunlight stirs the sea, trawling webs of bright lustre,
and the squall rides its white horses out into the bay.

Notes and acknowledgements

The title of each poem comes from one of the bays on the Pen-caer Peninsula, the far west of Pembrokeshire, known to the English as Strumble Head, moving west and south from Fishguard to St David's. (Allowing for fractals, some poems live a mile or two inland). OS map OL 35 refers. Other poems about Strumble Head, and some fuller accounts of the legends, may be found in my first collection, *Lodestone* (Stairwell Books, 2016).

Grateful thanks to Cathy and Mike Kurtz at Pwll Deri, in whose holiday cottage I have so often written poetry after days of walking the coastal path, to Simon Coton, who shares and feeds my passion for the wilder corners of Wales, and Patrick Lodge and Clare Wigzell who read many drafts of some of the poems.

Abergwaun I- III
Abergwaun (Fishguard) was the location for filming both *Under Milk Wood* and *Moby Dick*. In the Town Hall hangs the Last Invasion tapestry which records the unsuccessful attempt by a French expeditionary force to conquer Britain in 1797.

Nanhyfer – a diversion via St Non's
The cuckoo is on the RSPB 'red' list of endangered birds. See *Watch the Birdie*, ed. Rebecca Bilkau (Beautiful Dragons, 2018). Matthew 16.18 refers.

Pant y Dŵr, Porthsychen, Pwll Deri
Two times of year are especially good for seal watching on this coast; April when the seals emerge to mate, and September when they bring their pups onto the beaches. *Pant y Dŵr* was previously published in *The Curlew.*

Aber Felin I. Llanwnda, Careg Samson, Pwll Olfa
West Wales abounds with prehistoric remains, many offering dramatic views of the sea.

Carreg Onnen
Wild ponies are protected in this area as their grazing helps maintain the ecosystems.

Pwll Deri I-II. Sŵn y morloi means 'sound of the seals'.

Aber Bach hosts a holiday
An earlier version of this poem was published in *Sarasvati*, Autumn 2018.

Melin Tregwynt – a spin-off
The mill has operated for centuries and been run by the same family since 1912. Five mills were once fed by the nameless stream which powers the water wheel. See also Genesis 22.13.

Aber Mawr The first couple of lines refer to Matthew Arnold's poem, *On Dover Beach*.

Beacon – a diversion
A 'cone of confusion' is a zone of indeterminism over a navigational beacon such as a VOR (a rotating directional signal transmitted from the ground), allowing passing aircraft to pinpoint their location. MH370 Malaysian Airlines Boeing 777 went missing 8 March 2014 en route from Kuala Lumpur to Beijing.

Abercastle
Abercastle was previously published as *'Land Ahoy'* in *Lodestone*. It owes its genesis to the inscription engraved on a grey slate plaque at Abercastle Harbour: 'Alfred 'Centennial' Johnson, First Single Handed Atlantic Sailing West to East in a Fishing Dory, Gloucester, Mass, USA to Abercastle, Wales, June 15th – August 10th, 1876'.

Abereiddi
The winter storms of 2013/14 consumed 5 metres of the harbour overnight. The Blue Lagoon was a slate quarry, from which vast quantities of slate were transported by tram line.

About the author

Hannah Stone has been widely anthologised and published on ezines and in print journals including Algebra of Owls, The North, Poetry Salzburg Review, Prole and Orbis. Solo publications include *Lodestone* (Stairwell Books, 2016) and *Missing Miles* (Indigo Dreams, 2017), which won the Geoff Stevens Memorial Prize.
Collaborations include *An After Dinner's Sleep* and *Holding up Half the Sky* (Indigo Dreams, 2015 and 2019). She collaborates with composers, poets and broadcasters. Her Penthos Requiem with Matthew Oglesby had its premiere in 2018 (penthos.uk). She convenes the poets/composers forum for the Leeds Lieder festival and comperes WordSpace, a regular spoken word event in Leeds. In other lives she is a hill walker, forager, singer and teacher. A Londoner, she has lived in Leeds for 30 years but now considers West Wales her second home.